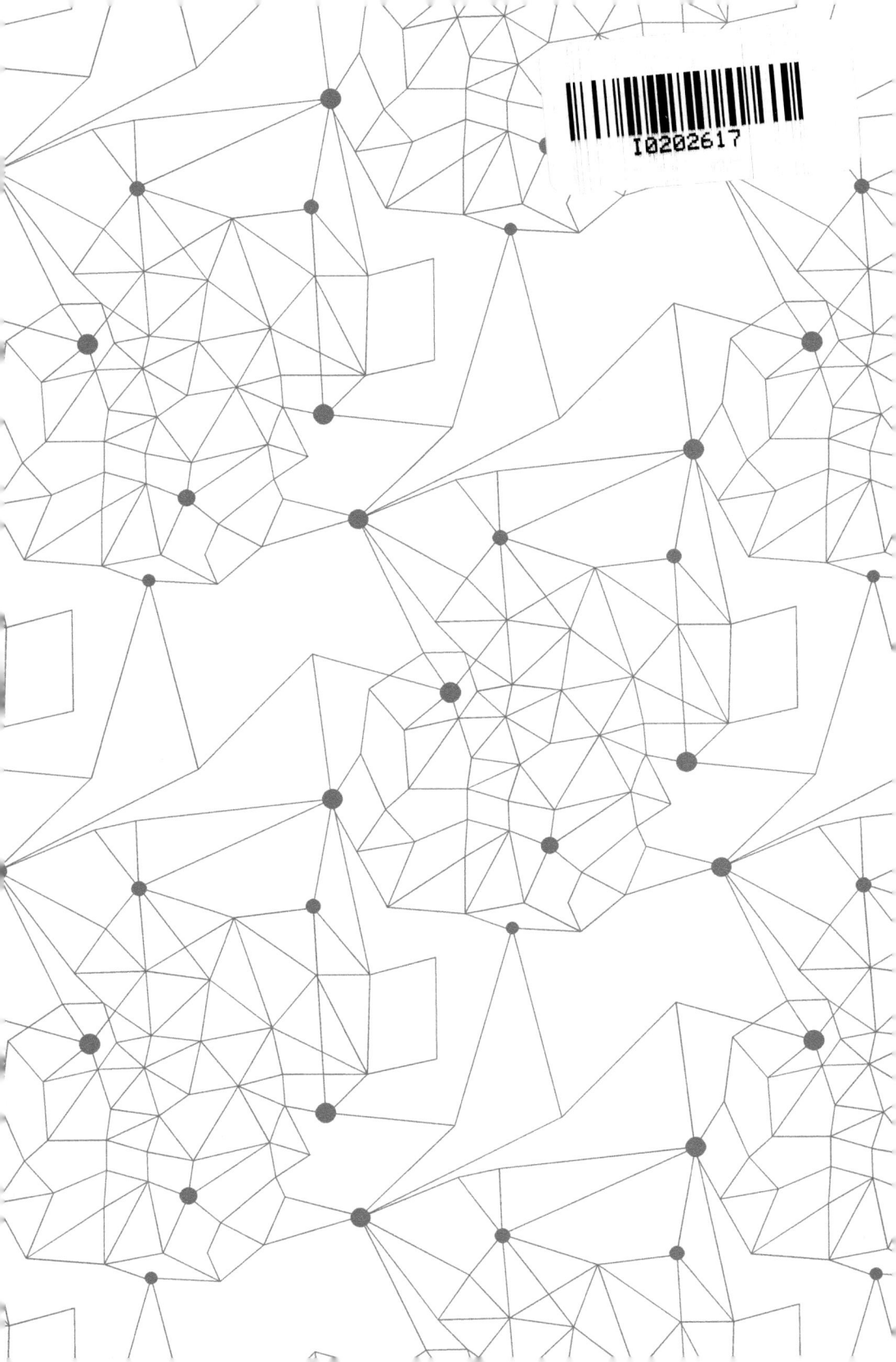

Dedication

For my family in blood
And my family in words

Listen
To the words Soul asks you to transcribe
You and you alone
You and not you
At the same time

Take the dictation
Of the spirit that speaks in your voice

This poetry is ours,
I have no doubt

Look up
To the sky

Table of Contents

We Finally Confront the Lie

The Naming of Real Things 8
Hidden in Our Hearts 9
It Starts So Young, This Hatred of Women 10
She Will Be Here Long After Us 12
Difficult 13
Sleep Like A Baby 15
Do You Feel More Powerful Now? 18
He Didn't Have To Hit Me 20
They Must Be Afraid of Our Blood 21
Not in My Name 24
Photographs of My Father 25
Get Bigger 27
Love More 29

We Must Keep the Children Safe

Who Am I Now? 32
Captain 34
Mother Love 36
I Saw a World 37
Talking With My Son About God 38
Here in This Moment 39
Well-Meaning 41
It Comes in Waves 42
Things I Know You Can Do 43
Prayer 44
Resting 45

We Honor the Land in Song

Here We Stand 48
Love and Jasmine 50
Yet To Be Told 51
The River That Shouldn't Be There 52
They Didn't Count on Us 53
My Heart Aches for My Homeland 55
Quiet 57
Spring 58
She Calls To Us 59

We Know How to Find Our Worth

Foundations of Love and Resistance 62
Suprised by This Body... 64
Mother/Daughter 66
You Talk Too Much.. 67
The Back Row.. 69
Houdini.. 70
Muscle Memory 72
Wild.. 73
Never 75
Value 76
I'm Giving Up 77
I Want... 79

We Finally
Confront the Lie

The Naming of Real Things

The opposite of gaslighting
Is poetry,
The naming of real things

I write it down
So it exists
I speak it
So you can't change it

I have no doubts.

I know
What really happened
I know
What is true
I know
What I did
I know
What you did too

I can see just fine, thank you.

Hidden in Our Hearts

We've weaponized our fear to hurt others.

But what is it that hides in our hearts
And makes us so afraid
That we've decided
Someone simply being themselves
Is a threat to our own selfhood?
Have we cut ourselves off
From our humanity so fully
We mistake our fear for righteousness?
So certain our pain is someone else's fault.

This is our great lie—
Intellectualism is not armor
Isolation is not protection
Elitism is not redemptive
Nationalism will not save us
Fragility is not Grace
Phobia will not free us

Once we crush
Everyone
Different
(And therefore dangerous),
There will be no one left to blame.
And we'll finally,
Finally have to confront the lie
That sits in our own hearts,

Our fear of ourselves
Is infinitely more dangerous
Than which bathroom
Or which water fountain
A person uses.

It Starts So Young,
This Hatred of Women

It starts so young,
this hatred of women

A bunch of nine-year-old boys
after baseball practice.
One of them has a scooter,
another says *Eww, it's pink*
and starts to prance and mince his steps
affecting some strange flamingo-like posture,
mocking the feminine.

It starts so young,
this hatred of women

Eighteen, a pile of friends
asleep on the basement couch.
I wake up to a boy who is not my boyfriend
fondling my breast.
I lie completely still.
I don't know what to do.
And my first thought
isn't to slap him and move away,
that would be mean.
My first thought
is to consider if I do in fact want this boy,
who has taken a piece of my body
without asking,
to be my boyfriend.
As if taking something of mine
obligates me to become yours.

It starts so young,
this hatred of women

But my son says to the boy
mocking femininity on the pink scooter
So what if it's pink?
So what if it's pink?

It starts so young

And my daughter
Oh my dearest glorious darling daughter
I see you choose yourself every day—
short hair because you love it,
a pile of science books by your bed,
never one for dolls.
Trying to figure out who you are
in a world that says
girls are one thing
and one thing only.
And you, my daughter,
my dearest glorious darling daughter,
you know
you are so many, many things.

It starts so young
You know
You refuse
Unwilling to be defined
Unwilling to be contained

She Will Be Here Long After Us

My whole life
I have come to the ocean
For healing and balm

She has held me close
And washed me clean

Today though,
I find no peace
As her waves break on the shore

For the first time
She has no healing words for me
No relief

Her energy is relentless, insistent
Full of acid and rage

She will be here
Long after us

She knows the fate
We write for ourselves

She knows
And is not sorry

Difficult

— adjective
1. not easily or readily done; requiring much labor, skill, or planning to be performed successfully; hard

I labored with you
for over fourteen hours.
Stalling for hours
at four centimeters.

I have a difficult time being out of control.

2. hard to understand or solve

Your grandfather took too many pills
and died.
You never met him.
But we knew we could no longer ignore
your rage.
We needed to understand.

An accurate diagnosis was difficult.
The therapist said it was a mood disorder.
Two psychiatrists agreed.
We prepared ourselves for that future
while we waited the long three months
for our appointment with the third doctor.

She's not bipolar,
he said.
ADHD looks different in girls.

3. hard to deal with or get on with

For the first three years of your life
your father and I were only married
because we were married.
We couldn't get on with each other.
I was drowning.
He was too.

But neither of us knew
how to reach the other.
Our voices locked
inside our gendered roles,
the ache difficult to articulate,
more difficult still to bear.

4. hard to please or satisfy

Your grandfather was a hard man to please.
A broken man
who tried to break others,
like his father before him.
Men filling their wounds
by stealing from the next generation.
Never satisfied.

And for years
it was difficult to tell
if I was wounding you as well.

5. hard to persuade or induce; stubborn

I want to raise a stubborn daughter.

I want the world
to be powerless
to persuade her
away from herself.

May she know the power
of being
a difficult woman.

Sleep Like a Baby

Once my mom told me,
If you have kids,
take a moment
to watch them sleep
at the end of the hard days.
It will melt the day's struggles
back into love.

At eighteen or so
I was surprised to learn
that sometimes
she needed such moments
with me.

In that moment
I saw her as a person,
not just Mom.
I saw deeper
into all the ways she loved me.
For there was more to her than me,
but nothing meant more to her
than me.

***

After the divorce
I still had to spend
every other Saturday night
at my father's house,
even though I didn't want to.

I slept on the couch in the living room.
On occasion
I would wake
to him standing there
camera in hand.

I always hated
when he took pictures of me,

but those were the worst.
Never indecent,
and yet,
I felt over exposed.

I am glad he's dead.

***

You know what?
"Sleep like a baby"
is some straight up
bullshit.

My oldest did not sleep
in any sort of reliable way
for the first fifteen months of her life.
I thought I was going to die
from sleep deprivation,
uncertainty,
and the anxiety
of never knowing
when,
or for how long,
I might be able to be more
than just Mom
and escape back into myself
while she slept.

***

The younger one,
born on the larger side,
always slept just fine.

Of course I don't have a favorite,
but I was healed
by his easy sleep.

***

And now
here I am,
and sometimes I can't help
but grab my phone
to take a picture of each
before I wake them up for school.

They are unspeakably beautiful
in that moment
at the threshold
between sleep
and morning.

I'm glad I take after my mother.

Do You Feel More Powerful Now?

Do you feel more powerful now
Having killed a young boy
Shot into his car window
On his way home from that party
So clearly a threat
To himself and others

Do you feel more powerful now
Having killed a young man
His loose cigarettes a real threat
To these criminal streets

Do you feel more powerful now
Having killed that shadowy figure
Hoody up, walking home
The neighbors needed you
To watch out for that one

Do you feel more powerful now
That she "killed herself"
After being taken downtown
Her tail light broken
Her rage clearly a criminal offense

Do you feel more powerful now
Having killed hundreds of our black
Brothers and sisters and sons and daughters
And husbands and wives and aunts and uncles
And grandparents and grandchildren
Over these hundreds and hundreds of years

Do you feel more powerful now
Having killed their bodies
In hundreds of ways?
Having criminalized their bodies
Over hundreds of days?
But sure, their music, their hairstyles
Look kinda ok
On your body

Do you feel more powerful now
Having killed—
I take that back—
Having tried to kill their spirits
By breaking their backs
Under the weight of your power
And yet you must know
There is a power within
That you will never touch

And what of the scared child within you
Who still believes the monster in the closet is real
And not a trick to keep you afraid?
Have you killed him too?

Do you feel more powerful now?

He Didn't Have To Hit Me

He didn't have to hit me
to keep me
in line

His soft words
tied me down
just fine

They Must Be Afraid of Our Blood

They must be afraid of our blood.

Not the blood of veins,
Which they are only too happy to spill

But the blood called by the moon
Spilling from between our legs

They say we are
Not to be touched
Unclean
Dangerous

I woke up to the roommate
On his knees on the bathroom floor
Rubber gloves and bleach
Meticulously cleaning the toilet.

I must have spilled some blood on the seat
Having left the light off
While changing my tampon
In the middle of the night.

If I had seen it
I would have wiped it up
In a swipe
Without giving it a second thought.
No bleach.
But he was afraid of my blood
Disgust in his eyes,
And wouldn't let me clean it up
When I offered.

Not to be touched
Unclean
Dangerous

And now they seek to legislate
And regulate
Everything
That comes from
Or comes with
Our blood

They must be afraid of our blood

But we have come to know our blood
In many ways
Over these many years.
It is of us
And we are not afraid of what we bring forth.

We bleed and we wash our hands
We bleed and we go to work
We bleed and we wash our legs
We bleed and we run and sleep and jump and have sex
We bleed and we wash our sheets
We bleed and we write poetry

And then
At times
We do not bleed.
And our blood transforms
What was half
Into a new whole.
New life
From our blood.

And then
At other times
We do not bleed.
We become
The elders.
New wisdom
As our blood dries.

At every phase
Its wisdom innate
Powerful
Holy

Vast
Deep
Unstoppable
Persistent
The world made and remade
Through our blood, flow, and Life.

And they can't stand it.
They don't understand it.
They can't have it.
So they tell everyone it is bad—
We are bad—
Because we bleed.
Not to be touched
Unclean
Dangerous

You may be afraid of our blood
You may be disgusted by Life

But
We
Are
Not.

We raise our voices
Refuse to hide our blood
Refuse to be ashamed

Our blood washes away the old
Our blood nourishes the new
We are not afraid of flow
We are not afraid of Life

It is time now
For us all
To return
To the blood.
To embrace
The deep red
Source flow
That birthed us all.

Not in My Name

Stop putting my name on your bombs.
You do not get to take my power and claim it for your own.

No!

Keep my name off your lips while you kill our children.

For shame!

Death does not come in my name.
I spill no blood but in the name of birth.

You dishonor my name when you claim
Your bombs protect our children.
I who have carried them within my body
Their potential impact greater than any bomb.
And yet you bomb them and name it Peace.
The blast radius extends for a mile in every direction.

No!

I will not sign my name
To your excuse note.
You excuse of a man.
If you can do this,
You have forgotten my face.
You cannot claim greatness.
Not again.
Not ever.

You have forgotten the name of your mother.

Photographs of My Father

He died in March
and I didn't want to look at his stupid face
ever again.

But I had to know.

I had to know what drew people to him.
I had to know if there was good in him.
I had to know, am I like him?

Echoes of myself
look back at me
across the years.

In this picture
his glasses
are almost exactly the same
as the pair I wear.
And so we must,
at least in some small way,
have the same
face shape
sense of style
lens on the world.

Were he still alive,
I would not want to see this truth.
But now,
it is a surprising comfort—
a connection to lineage I didn't know I had.

For here he stands in the office doorway
absentmindedly rubbing the nail of his right ring finger
with the pad of his right thumb
while he's thinking,
Just like me.

Here he stands in front of a hotdog stand
in a full beard of red hair and a bright orange jumpsuit.

In the same moment a *fuck you* to convention
and a longing to belong,
Just like me.

Here he stands in a captain's hat and tie-dyed shirt
his wares laid out on a blanket
on the ground at the flea market.
He is such a weirdo,
Just like me.

Here he stands, talking with his hands
eyes on fire
smile so wide
as he talks about something
he was making or
he cared about or
he loved,
Just like me.

Here he stands looking straight into the camera
a little defiant
a little wounded
totally open,
Just like me.

And here he dances with my mother
when they were still together,
before they decided
they wanted me.

Get Bigger

My heart is collapsing
I can't hold the weight any more

Get bigger

I feel alone
Isolated

Get bigger

My work isn't working

Get bigger

My voice won't carry

Get bigger

I am afraid

Get bigger

I feel hopeless
What can one person do?

Get bigger

My magic is weak

Get bigger

I can barely breathe

Get bigger

Not a colonial bigness that takes
What doesn't belong to it,
Bulldozes and consumes and destroys.
No, not this.

Big like ocean
Big like wind
Big like cosmos
Big like mother's lap

Big enough to hold a heart
That will no longer believe the lie
That says I am too small
And will always be too small.

I can't change the size of the problem
Or the weight of the load.

I can expand
To carry it.

Get bigger.

Love More

Love more fully.
Let your love fill in all the cracks
Like Japanese gold.
Raise your heart
To your lips and drink till you are full.

Love more widely.
Let your love widen beyond all the borders
Inflicted by man.
Raise your arms
To the sky in blessings spread wide.

Love more deeply.
Let your love deepen beneath the surface
Of skin and kin and the way we each choose to worship.
Raise your eyes
To see the raw humanity standing before you, pain and wisdom so deep.

Love more fiercely.
Let your love rage like fire and do not be silent.
Raise your voice
To power again and again, unflinching and fierce.

Love more wildly.
Let your love wild like flowers blanketing a meadow in the spring.
Raise your feet
To dance among the blossoms, growing wild.

Love more warmly.
Let your love warm the icicles of contempt that pierce your heart.
Raise your glass
To the fountain of hope until your cup runneth over, sweet and warm.

Love more freely.
Let your love free from the small box you were told would keep it safe.
Raise your hands
To pick the locks and set yourself free.

We Must Keep
the Children Safe

Who Am I Now?

Who am I now that I have become a mother?
I am tears in the middle of the night,
forgotten lunch boxes,
mismatched socks.

I am lawyer, doctor, confidant, chef,
secretary, peacekeeper, chauffeur.

I am insider outsider.
Alone and never alone.

I am wise and full of doubt.
Powerless and the place where the buck stops.

I am wide lap and smoothed hair and dried tears.

I am endurance past imagining,
exhaustion beyond sleeping,
overwhelm past sanity.

I am paralyzed and powerful.
I am destroyed and made new
made new
made new.

I am love beyond words
beyond time
beyond reason
and all of the stars.

I am hope and fear and laughter
snot and blood
missing sneakers
found in the laundry basket.

I am *clean up the playroom,*
eat your vegetables,
remember your water bottle,
and *push in your chair.*

I am the unlocked door
when you run away from home again.

I am buffeted and unwavering,
fearless and terrified,
measuring short
measuring short
measuring short.

I am lullabies
and late night, past your bedtime snuggles.

I am language and rhythm and flow and joy.

I am the found voice,
free after years of silence.

I am gatekeeper, guide, and guardian.

I am *Twinkle Twinkle*
and *You Are My Sunshine*
and *Zippity Do Dah*.

I am everything and nothing at all.

I am poems
written on my phone in the dark
without my glasses on.

I am open ears, open eyes, open arms, open lap.

You are my child
my teacher
my spirituality
my practice
my heart.

I am your mother.

Captain

Waking up yesterday she says
I dreamt I was the captain of a Starship.
So real to her.
Filled with pride.
Imagination on fire.

At recess
she organized her friends to play space explorers.
Home again,
she conscripts family members to dress up with her.

She named her ship *Journey*,
and all day she flew among the stars.

Last night, way past lights out,
Mom can I talk to you?
No. Please stop stalling and go to bed.

I brush my teeth.
Lay down in bed.
Sigh.
Get up and return to her room.
I must always listen
even if the timing makes me tired.

Standing in her doorway in the dark,
Mom? This morning it was so real,
but now it's starting to fade away.
She rests her head against my chest.

I bend my head only slightly to kiss the top of her head.
She is so tall now.
I kiss the wool of the beanie she's wearing to bed,
her current obsession with them not limited to daytime hours.
She is trying on so many different identities at once.

I say,
You will have so many ways to make it real again:
Write a story.

Use that brain of yours to become an engineer
and build your own starship.
There are so many ways for you to be a captain,
but now it's time to get some sleep.

I love you.

Mother Love

I can find words for everything
But I cannot find words to talk about my mom.

Never think I don't love her.

But know that my love for her formed before
My tongue knew how to form words,
Back, back, back, even to the very forming of my tongue itself.

There is no breath I have taken on this earth
That has not breathed with my love of her.
There will be no breath I take upon this earth
That will not be filled with my love of her.
My body knows it breathes because of her.

So how then could I find the one right word
When her cells sit at the source of every word.

I Saw a World

Yesterday I saw
a world of stories
in the faces
of my sleeping children
before they woke.

Talking With My Son About God

He's the quiet one.
The one whose speech slows him down.
So many words come out at once,
Sometimes the sense gets muddled.
So we just are.
Together without words.

His grandma mentioned to me the other day
That he wanted to know about God.
We haven't talked about it.
Wanted him to have the space
To make up his own mind.

So there
In the housewares aisle
I ask him
If he believes in God.

Yes,
He says.
Why?
I ask.
Because I was thinking about life
And how it has to come from somewhere.

I know the feeling, kid.
The only word
For hearing the first heartbeat
Is miraculous.

Here in This Moment

Today your anxiety flared up again
in almost all the same old ways.
Demanding
then refusing
all help.
Constant stream of words and arguments.
Lashing out.
So angry
on the surface.

But now I see
your fear
your overwhelm.
You fight against *not enough*
time
your belief in yourself.
You wind yourself up more and more
marshaling your defenses
against a threat
only you can see.

This time though,
I hold the boundary.
You feel what you need to feel.
I'll do what I need to do.
I love you.
And because I love you,
I will only do so much.
And because I love you,
I will only take so much,
only let you go so far,
before I say no.

I send you upstairs now for an early bedtime.
I hate you! you scream.
And then immediately,
I'm sorry. I didn't mean that.

As you head upstairs, yelling turns to tears.

And here in this moment is the miracle,
this turning back to yourself
to me
to us.
This has never happened before
you finding your own way back
from this far away.

Some parenting book I read said
the shift from anger to tears is an important one.
Normally those books are garbage,
but today I am grateful for this sign.

I know other parenting books would say
never back down from enforcing a rule
never let yourself be manipulated by tears.

But I know
without hesitation
that now we need to be together.

I'm up the stairs a few seconds behind you
gather all five feet of you in my lap
hold you tight
kiss your tears
It's ok. I've got you.

So grateful that you'll let me help you.
That you'll let me in.

Well-Meaning

*You can't change
someone else,
you can only change
yourself.*

*If you change
how you behave,
you can change
the relationship.*

The adults who speak
these words
mean well.
They mean them as
freedom.

But it depends.

If you're a child
whose father is ill,
these words
make you think
you can do something
to make him better.

And
if
you
just
keep
changing
and
changing
and
changing
yourself,
you will (have to eventually) find
the one way of being
that will make him well,
that will make him stop
making you cry.

It Comes in Waves

One minute
you're snuggling
with your children
before the day begins.

The next
a kind friend
sends you kind words
that touch a place inside you
that still aches.

And you cry
sitting on the floor of your closet
as you gently pull the small
scared child inside you
onto your lap.

We must keep the children safe.

Things I Know You Can Do

Why won't you help me?
She yells, tears streaming.

My darling
I will not help you
Do the things I know
You can do for yourself.

I probably will not help you
Do the things I'm not sure
You can do by yourself
Either.

But I will always be here.

Prayer

Today, the only thing my heart longs to say
Is a prayer for this world:

We all are so broken.
We all are so beautiful.
We each are so messy.
We each are so miraculous.

Please,
With my whole swelling heart
I beg,
No more
Bombs or guns or weapons of war.

We all long
To hug our children in the morning.

Resting

Your child's small,
warm hand
resting
on your cheek.

What else
is it time for
but this?

We Honor the
Land in Song

Here We Stand

Here we stand
Monsoon season
On the horizon

Old ways
We turned a color-blind eye to
Coming into the light,
We see them
And say *No More.*
Water wash us clean.

Here we stand

Even older ways
Returning to our hands,
Soul and story
And meaning remembered,
Soothing the ache of our forgetting.
Water for the parched heart.

Monsoon season
On the horizon

New ways
Created together,
New stories
Woven from every voice,
New systems
Wrought from renewed love.
Water of Life.

Here we stand

And I pray:

Wash the hate from our hearts
Wash the contempt from our eyes
Wash the blood from our hands
Wash the abuse from our lips

Monsoon season
On the horizon

Bathe our hearts in honeysuckle
Bathe our eyes in dew
Bathe our hands in swirls of fresh paint
Bathe our lips in the language of belonging

Here we stand
Monsoon season
On the horizon
On the verge of a new becoming

Love and Jasmine

This morning I woke
having dreamt of jasmine,
lines of poetry forming
themselves on my lips
as I opened my eyes.

My love and I together
shopping for travel treasures—
books to bring home
and plants that might survive the desert heat.

I can't remember the last time
I've had a good dream
I can remember upon waking.

Most nights I dream of
searching and searching
and searching
for someone I love
but I'm never
ever able to reach,
Or that a lost love
would have loved me again
if only I'd done this one thing
revealed in the dream,
Or that I've done the one thing
for which my love would leave me.

A miracle then
to dream in poetry
of true love
and jasmine.

Yet To Be Told

In a house that's not my own
I wait for the day's poem
to make itself known to me.

The little girl,
also not mine,
giggles
as her mother chases her
'round the deck,
while her father
sits at the piano,
searching
for the theme to a story
that has yet to be told.

The trees rustle,
and though I'll be driving away
from the ocean,
I am ready
to come home.

The River That Shouldn't Be There

This river used to flow regularly
But it is now dry,
Except on days like these—
A surprise blessing
Of flowing water
In the desert
After a weekend of heavy rain

Sitting on the river bank
Running my hands
Through rocky sand,
I look down
Shocked to discover
My skin covered in flecks sparkling gold.

I cannot have discovered gold.
This cannot possibly be gold on me.

And yet,
I don't feel the Fool
Seeing my body covered in gold
Shining in the sun,
As the river
That shouldn't be here
Flows at my feet.

Who knows
What treasures might rest
On the palm of your hand
At the side of the river
Made by rain?

They Didn't Count on Us

Though they try,
with their deluge of bad
Real News,
to knock us over,
to drown us out,
a flash flood sent
to wipe our feet out from under us
and rip out our roots,
they didn't count on us.

They didn't count on us
knowing what they're up to
seeing through their plan
calling them out
calling them on the phone
everyday.
They didn't count on us
refusing to stay silent,
saying *No.*

For we know who we are.
We know what we value.
We will not be swayed from our purpose.
We will not participate in our own drowning.

I've almost drowned a few times already.
I bet you have too.
And each time we learned which way was high
and which way was low.
We found our feet
and lifted our heads above the water line.

They thought they could catch us,
pull us under again.

But they didn't know that by almost drowning
we became the water,
covering 71 percent of the Earth,

sacred source of Spirit,
of Life.

They didn't count
on the songs of salt and stream
singing in our veins.
They didn't guess
our deep rivers reach
toward each other
toward Justice
toward Love.

They didn't know
we are the water.

My Heart Aches for My Homeland

My heart aches for my Homeland
Land of palm tree and sand
Land of hula and song
Land of plumeria, *pikake*, and ginger
Land of honor
Land of wisdom
Land of spirit

She is not the land of my ancestors.
My grandparents arrived by ocean liner
Twenty years before statehood

I am outsider
Other
Different
White
Foreign

And yet the Land holds me
Caress of wind
Blessing of rain
Ripe papaya, mango, banana
Offerings of life
Entwined in soul
Loving
Generous

We went barefoot to school
We honored the Land in song
We dug in Her dirt and climbed Her trees
We built model canoes from Her wood,
Wrapped offerings to the gods in Her *ti* leaves,
And cooked our food in Her sand.
We learned to love Her
With the souls of our feet,
The lilt of our voices,
And the work of our hands.

I left home at eighteen
For college and the world beyond.
I took Her for granted.
When I return, no one recognizes me.

But my feet remember
And my heart aches for my Homeland

We think we shape the Land,
But it is She who wears down our rough edges
And holds us in the palm of Her hand.

Quiet

House quiet
after a long holiday weekend
full of family of birth and choice.
Napping in a sunbeam on the couch.
Eyes closed,
the tree outside the window
casts shadows that shift across my face.
My daughter,
sitting next to me doing homework,
reaches out
smooths my brow
kisses my forehead.

Spring

After eleven years
Living in the desert,
The land has unfurled itself
After a winter
Of drenching rains.
The mountains
And washes are ablaze,
Blanketed with
The yellow blossoms
Of desert sage.

After sixteen years
With my husband,
I have finally learned
To let myself be loved.

She Calls To Us

Stand with me on the edge
Of the yearly Burn
Outer heat, inner heat
Rise together by degrees
The bushes brown
Blue skies bleach to white

She calls to us—
Let go
Let go
Let it all go.
You can not quench my fire
My fire burns in you.
There is nothing to be done
But to burn and be burned.
Lay your aching heart in mine
And trust.
I will take you
Right to the very edge.
Burn what must burn
And hold you all the while.

In the desert
Summer's heat
Everything meaningless burns away.
What remains is her gift
Hot
Pure
Elemental
Resilient
Golden
Alchemy of chaparral, Monsoon, and dust

Only love remains
As we await the drenching rain

We Know How to
Find Our Worth

Foundations of Love and Resistance

Because we have been abused
We know how to stop cycles of abuse.
Because we have been silenced
We know how to make a powerful noise.
Because we have been told
Over and over
How unworthy they think we are
We know how to find our worth
In the true voice of our own heart.

We've been here before
We know our way home

Name the patterns at play
Refuse to participate
Shape the words with your mouth
Shape the words with your pen
It really happened
Don't turn away
Freedom comes from naming what is true

Claim what happened to you
As the birthing ground of your power.
Heal yourself and know
You have different choices,
Different ways of relating
Than the ones that hurt you.

See clearly those who walk with you
Give them the space they need
To be fully who they are
Let them love you
Feel the love
Allow it all the way in
Put your energy here,
Into this foundation of love

We will make mistakes
Despite our best efforts
But this foundation of love
Of clearly seeing each other
Is where we put all our energy
So that when the storm comes
We are strong enough in our connection
Stable enough in our action
Deeply rooted enough in our conviction
To weather it without collapsing

Because we have been broken
We grew back stronger

This is what we've been training for
This is where we put every ounce of our attention
This is what we build together

Surprised by This Body

I never look at myself in the mirror.
My own femininity
Something I've chosen not to see.

But the other day
I caught a glimpse of my naked body—
Almost forty,
Arms raised while brushing my hair.

She doesn't look like she used to.
I thought the one gift
Of small boobs
Was that at least they wouldn't sag.
The skin around my belly button
Rumpled and puckered
From expanding and contracting
To hold my children.
Everything too soft, too loose, too large.

And yet,
Today I see her differently.
I am surprised to see this body of mine
Is the body of a goddess.
Not the Goddess of Vogue,
But fertile Ishtar, Bridgid, Frejya, Demeter.

Depicted not in the fullness of youth
Or the fullness of being with child
But later
After her body filled and emptied
Filled and emptied.
And now she stands,
Low breasts, wide hips, full belly
Soft, large, and round
Grounded by the weight of Mother Earth
Nourishing what she has made.
And for the first time
I stop

To look in the mirror a while
And be blessed
By all the weights
My heart has shed
And all the weights
My body has carried.

Mother/Daughter

I love my daughter
let's get that out on the table
right away

And

It is hard for me
to love my daughter

Not for herself—
she is wild rain in the desert
and the smell of creosote

It is hard to love
the wholeness I see in her
that reminds me
of the parts of myself
I find hard to love

And yet
I love her so completely
I see her soul clearly

And
she loves me so completely
she sees my soul clearly

And so
I come to love
these tender places.

Slowly.

You Talk Too Much

You talk too much
Always my first thought
When I meet someone new
Or when I'm in a class
Or when a dear friend calls

You talk too much
No one wants to hear you natter on
Who do you think you are?

You talk too much
In elementary school—
Reseated and reseated
Moved to the end of the row
Next to the super shy kid.
And still I talked
Too much

You talk too much
In high school English class
Pulled aside one day
And asked to give the other students
A chance to talk

You talk too much
Good girls, good people
Don't talk so much.
I was never told outright
That my worth and my silence
Were intertwined,
But that's what they meant

You talk too much
But I have so much to say
I am not shy
I know the answer
I know my thoughts
I know my mind
I get so excited

Words tumble out
I can't keep quiet
I can't help myself

I talk too much.
And you know what?
I am Loud
And you have to
Deal with that
And you know what?
My voice will change the world.

The Back Row

Women are supposed to be silent,
But I burned that memo.

And thank you for the offer,
But I've never needed a microphone
For my voice to reach the back row.

Houdini

I disappear when conflict comes.
Not like Houdini,
Though that would be more fun.
Instead I pack away
Everything that matters to me
So you cannot break it.
Pinch it tightly between my lips
So it cannot escape.
Lock it into the strong muscle of my heart
So you cannot deny it.
Close it in my belly
So you cannot see in my face
How much it matters to me.

It's a pattern well-worn—
If I don't want anything
You can't take it away at the last minute
Even though I upheld my end of the deal.
If I don't ask,
I can't be told
No no no no no no no no no
Until I disappear.
My wants can't be thrown back in my face,
Turned against me as weapons
More lethal because I made them myself
So they know just where and how to hurt me.

Giving my power away feels so normal
That I'll hand it to you myself
Without even noticing
And call it success.

I don't know where I stand
Unless I can see myself in you.

No more.

My lips
Speak my will

The strong muscle of my heart
Claims my space
My belly
Breathes life into what matters most
As I unfold all the places
Where I've hidden
And tucked my wanting away

Muscle Memory

I still have
muscle memory
of the years
when I lived Silent.
Held it all in,
bit my tongue,
and clenched my jaw
tight enough
to grind my teeth down
until they cracked.

That is not how my story ends.

I can't, won't,
slip silently backward
into that small,
airless box
again.

I am
no longer Silent.

I'd rather write poems
and rejoice,
out here
in this field
with you.

Wild

No
You cannot claim me
No
You can't come over
No
You can't call
No
Not just once more
No
Not just to talk
No
I am not yours
No
Your manipulation is not love
No
You cannot claim me
No

I am mine
My No
The first
Of many,
Many words
With which I free myself

My Yes
The first
Of many,
Many words
With which I claim myself

Yes
I am wild
Yes
I swim in the moonlight
Yes
I am a poet
Yes
I weave my Want into magic

Yes
I mother
Yes
I loved you before time began
Yes
I am a wife
Yes
I wrap my legs around love
Yes
I pull you close
Yes
Yes
Yes

Never

I've never worn your make up
Never slipped on your high heeled shoes

I've never kept my voice down
Or refused to sing my blues

I've never read your magazines
I look to my soul for clues

I've never drunk your alcohol
You can't buy my truth with booze

I've never watched your reality show
Won't be a sucker for your Fake News

I've never believed in your original sin
I'll fuck with whomever I choose

Value

I've spent so much
trying to sell shit
that wasn't for sale.

Waited for ages
for someone to say
Yes
to my voice
with their dollars,
all the while
falling more and more
Silent
in the Capital's shade.

I put price tags
on my heart,
asked you to buy it from me,
give me value.
Charge what you're worth!
As if money is the sole measure of the soul.

In the end
I'll give my story freely
for the chance
to meet you
here
under the stars
as the spring breezes blow.

I'm Giving Up

I'm giving up
Pushing boulders up mountains
I'm giving up
Trying to sell my soul
I'm giving up
Trying to be something
I never wanted to be in the first place,
And the voices that say I don't already know who I am

I'm giving up
Productivity
I'm giving up
Hacks
I'm giving up
Clicks and likes and links
I'm giving up
Hustling for the Algorithm's attention

I'm giving up
Self-help
I'm giving up
Listening to other people's gurus
I'm giving up
Giving up my power
To anyone who claims to know me
Better than I know myself

I'm giving up
Trying to earn a seat at your table
I'm giving up
Being the audience
For your branding
I'm giving up
What you're selling
I'm giving up
Empowerment
That comes with a price tag
On the back of another

I'm giving up
Measuring my worth
By checks on a list
Instead of the poems
I've written and lived

And the only speed I want to measure
Is how quickly I can reach your heart

I Want

With each passing day
I am coming to know
My Want

Oh sweet wonder of wanting

We are told we can't want
We are told it is ego
We learn to believe we can't want
We learn to believe we are wrong

Wanting is selfish
Wanting is bad
Wanting leaves us
Wanting more
Insatiable greed

But to deny Want
Is to disavow the clear language
Of the Soul

Oh the sweet boon of wanting

Steadfast companion
Faithful guide
Soul voice
Everyday gift

Wanting simply is

And
I want
Oh do I want

I want to make things.
Make things happen.

I want to heal and make whole.
I want to seal and protect.

I want to roar and disrupt and stand up.

I want to break what needs to be broken,
Rend what needs to be torn,
Shatter what needs to be cracked.

I want to strengthen what needs to be supported,
Defend what needs to be protected,
Shelter what needs to grow.

I want my voice to be louder than fear,
My heart stronger than hate,
My magic bigger than ego.

I want to know that the future is not fixed.
I want to navigate by Want.
I want to know that my individual actions matter
As we shape our humanity.

I want you to know you are not alone.

I want to make art and magic and power and story.
I want to make things with my hands and heart and words.
I want to be made useful, powerful, graceful, and precise.

I want my words to make new the world.
I want to dwell in Sovereignty.
I want peace that comes from knowing
Growing
Wielding my power.

I want to make things that make me feel alive.
I want to make and make and make.

Acknowledgements

Thank you to my sisters in art and words—Harmony, your invitation to write a poem every day and see what happens brought me to a deeper understanding of my process and a deeper knowing that poetry is for me. Staci, you called forth many of these words. Layla, thank you for helping me see it was time to get this book out in the world and for the word witchery of your beautiful blessing. Andrea, your paintings help me see my way into new words. Julie, your poems asked the questions that lit the way. Jena, thank you for helping me birth this book through your fierce encouragement and loving editing. Karen, thank you for long walks and long conversations about how to tell the best stories. KK, you're awesome.

Thank you to Desiree Adaway for the right words at the right time (*Resting*), to Leigh Steele for calling for a love of desert heat (*She Calls to Us*), and Roxane Gay for the invitation to be difficult (*Difficult*).

Thank you to Jenn and the Radical Relating crew for introducing me to my Want and my Will.

Thank you Sutton for seeing my heart and helping me make it tangible.

To Tessa, Mallory, and Káren, your love across the years and across the miles always helps me find my way home.

To my family. My love for you fills every syllable.

About the Author

Miki DeVivo is a poet and storyteller who writes to foster change, turn us back toward each other, and remind us who we really are. Making space for more stories opens more room for us to be who we are, see ourselves clearly, and love more fully. Learn more about her work at www.mikidevivo.com.

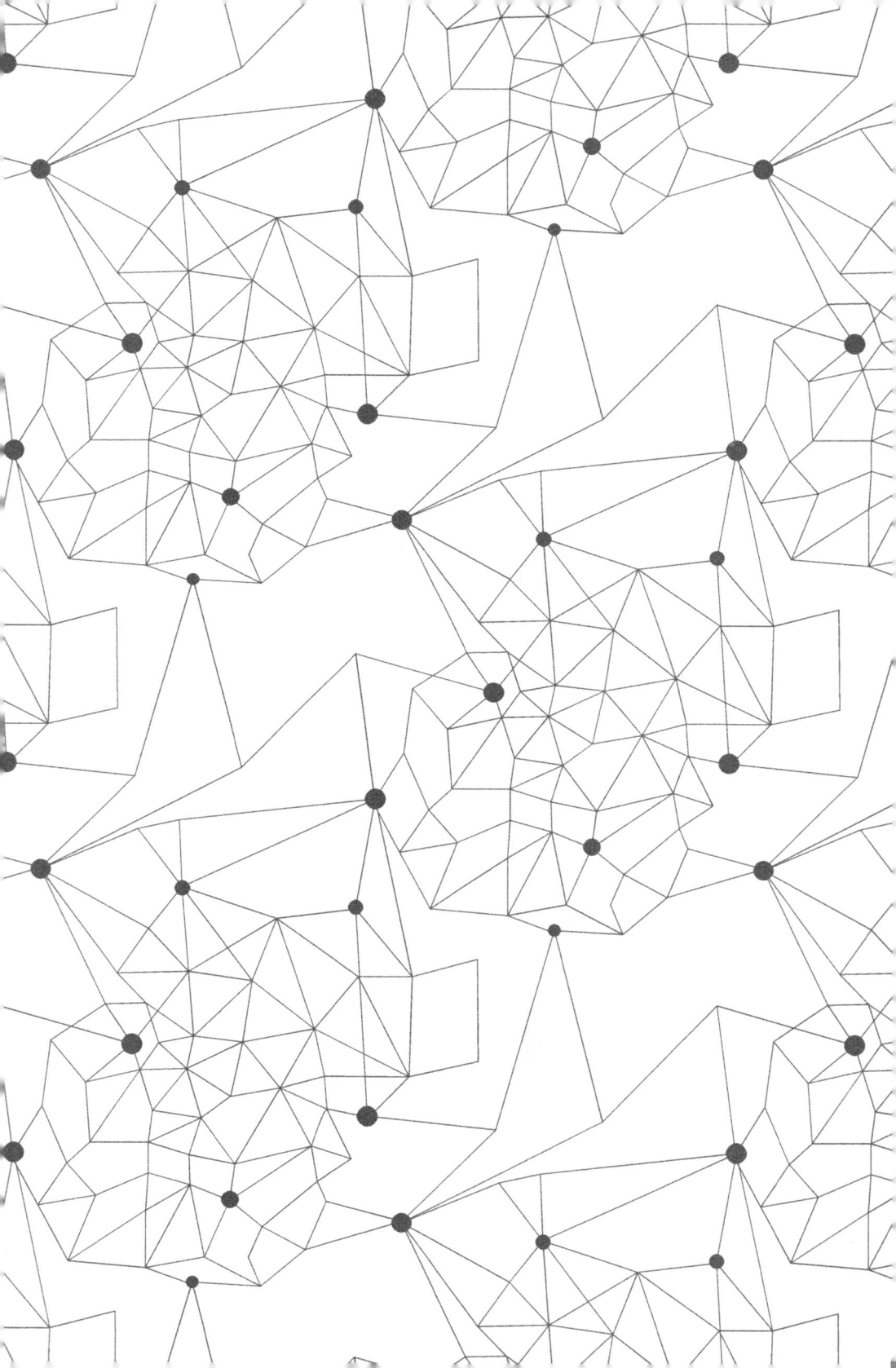

www.ingramcontent.com/pod-product-compliance
Lightning Source LLC
Chambersburg PA
CBHW070009100426

42741CB00012B/3165